Walt Disney's

MICKEY MOUSE ADVENTURES

TAKE-ALONG COMIC

GEMSTONE PUBLISHING

TIMONIUM, MARYLAND

STEPHEN A. GEPPI
*President/Publisher and
Chief Executive Officer*

JOHN K. SNYDER JR.
Chief Administrative Officer

STAFF

LEONARD (JOHN) CLARK
Editor-in-Chief

GARY LEACH
Associate Editor

SUE KOLBERG
Assistant Editor

TRAVIS SEITLER
Art Director

SUSAN DAIGLE-LEACH
Production Associate

DAVID GERSTEIN
Archival Editor

MELISSA BOWERSOX
Director-Creative Projects

• IN THIS ISSUE •

Mickey Mouse
All About Mickey
Story: Stefan Petrucha Art: Joaquin

Donald Duck
**Ring Thrice and I'll Clobber You,
My Lad**
Story: Mark Shaw Art: Bancells

Original interior color by **Egmont**
Lettering by **Jamison Services**
Additional production by **Gary Leach**

Mickey Mouse
The Imperial Vortex
Story: Rudy Salvagnini
Art: Graziano Barbaro
Translation and dialogue: Dwight Decker
Lettering: Rick Keene

Cover art by **Noel Van Horn** • Cover color by **Gary Leach**

ADVERTISING/ MARKETING

J.C.VAUGHN
Executive Editor

BRENDA BUSICK
Creative Director

JAMIE DAVID
Director of Marketing

SARA ORTT
Marketing Assistant

HEATHER WINTER
Office Manager
Toll Free
(888) 375-9800 Ext. 249
ads@gemstonepub.com

MARK HUESMAN
Production Assistant

MIKE WILBUR
Shipping Manager

RALPH TURNER
Staff Accountant

**WALT DISNEY'S
MICKEY MOUSE
ADVENTURES 7**
Take-Along Comic
December, 2005

Published by
Gemstone Publishing

ALL ABOUT MICKEY

MIRRORS ONLY SHOW WHAT'S IN FRONT OF THEM, RIGHT? WELL, SOME MAY HAVE MORE BEHIND THEM...

THIS IS THE *BEST* HOUSE OF MIRRORS I'VE EVER SEEN! HERE'S WHAT I'D LOOK LIKE IF I *ATE* MORE AND FELL UNDER A *PILE-DRIVER!* HA-HA!

D 99278

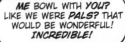

AS THE GAME PROGRESSES...

MAGIC MOUSE - 33
FLIP THE FISH - 18
MAGIC MOUSE - 31

OH, NO! *NO!*

I WANTED TO SCORE *EXACTLY* THE SAME AS MY HERO, MICKEY MOUSE! NOW ALL IS *LOST!* *HOPELESS!* NO, NO, NO!

MARTY, LOOK! I THINK YOU'RE TAKING THIS *FAN* THING TOO *FAR!* IT'S NOT WORTH GETTING *UPSET* OVER A SILLY SCORE!

GRRRR!

YOU'RE JUST BEING KIND! I'M A *FAILURE!* I DON'T *DESERVE* TO BE YOUR FAN! GOODBYE - *FOREVER!*

GOOFY, YOU'LL NEVER *BELIEVE* THIS, BUT MARTY JUST HAD A TANTRUM BECAUSE HE DIDN'T *SCORE* THE SAME AS I DID!

GAWRSH, MICKEY, TH' GUY'S JUST TRYIN' TA BE YER *PAL!* HE'S PROB'LY *SENSITIVE!* MAYBE YUH WERE TOO *HARD* ON 'IM!

NOW I FEEL *GUILTY!* I HOPE HE'S *OKAY!*

POOR GUY! THERE I GO, BEING *HARD* ON HIM AGAIN! HE'S JUST *SO* SENSITIVE!

BUT TO BE HONEST, I'M A LITTLE *RELIEVED!* HE REALLY *WAS* GIVING ME *TOO* MUCH ATTENTION!

MMMM! NO SENSE LETTING THIS TERRIFIC MEAL HE COOKED GO TO *WASTE*, THOUGH...

RATS! I JUST *INSULTED* THE GUY AND PRACTICALLY *KICKED* HIM OUT! I *CAN'T* EAT HIS FOOD!

HEY, BOY! WANT SOME YUMMY *POT ROAST?* YOUR FAVORITE!

SIGH! EVEN *PLUTO* THINKS I DID THE *WRONG* THING!

BY AND BY...

IT'S BEEN A FEW DAYS! I SHOULD GIVE MARTY A *CALL* TO APOLOGIZE! ON THE OTHER HAND, HE MAKES ME A LITTLE *NERVOUS*...

I'LL DROP IN AND MAKE SURE *MINNIE'S* STILL ON FOR THE *MOVIES* TONIGHT! *THEN* MAYBE I'LL CALL MARTY!

MINNIE MOUSE

OH, HI, MICKEY! *MARTY* DROPPED BY TO HELP ME WITH MY GARDENING! WASN'T THAT *SWEET?*

UH, YEAH, I GUESS! HOW ARE YOU, MARTY?

HE TOLD ME YOU WERE *MEAN* TO HIM, MICKEY! MAYBE YOU SHOULD *APOLOGIZE!*

WELL...*UM*, MAYBE I *WAS* A LITTLE RUDE, BUT *YOU* DID COME INTO MY *HOUSE* WITHOUT ASKING! HOW ABOUT... I APOLOGIZE IF *YOU* DO?

NO!

LATER...

PSHH! MAYBE I CAN FORGET MY TROUBLES BY *FISHING* WITH HORACE! WE'RE SUPPOSED TO MEET BY THE OLD TROUT STREAM!

HAWR-HAWR-HAWR! MARTY, YOU *ARE* A *CARD!*

HEH-HEH-HEH!

HEY, MICKEY - GLAD YOU COULD MAKE IT! MARTY WAS JUST TELLING ME ONE *FUNNY* STORY! HE'S A *GREAT* WIT!

UH...C'MERE, MICKEY, PAL! LET'S *TALK!*

GRR!

LOOK, IT'S OBVIOUS TO *ME* THAT MARTY, HERE, JUST WANTS TO MAKE *FRIENDS!* HE ADORES YOU! WHY ARE YOU BEING SO *TOUGH* ON HIM?

TOUGH? HE TRESPASSED AND WON'T APOLOGIZE-

OH! I *HEARD* HOW HE CLEANED YOUR *FILTHY* HOUSE FOR *FREE!* IF YOU HATE HIM *THAT* MUCH, YOU CAN FISH WITH SOMEONE *ELSE*, TODAY!

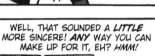

SHORTLY... THAT SHOULD BE WARM ENOUGH! BUT IF YOU NEED AN EXTRA BLANKET, THERE'S ONE IN THE CLOSET!

THANKS, MICKEY! YOU'VE BEEN A REALLY **GOOD** HOST!

I'LL BE OUTTA YOUR HAIR FIRST THING IN THE MORNING! YAWN! NOW FOR SOME SHUT-EYE!

HE **SEEMS** TO BE ACTING PERFECTLY **NORMAL** – I GUESS I'VE BEEN WORRIED FOR NOTHING! OH WELL, TIME FOR SOME SLEEP!

A SLEEP HAUNTED BY NIGHTMARES! WHAT CAN IT MEAN?

NO! **NO!** THE **MIRRORS** ARE **ALIVE!** SOMEONE **HELP** ME!

GOOD TO *SEE* YOU, MICKEY, BUT A LITTLE *SURPRISIN'!*

IS EVERYTHING GOING ACCORDING TO *PLAN?*

GASP!

I GET IT! THIS GANG THINKS *I'M* "MARTY" - THE MICKEY OF THEIR WORLD!

HMM! *OUR* PLUTO ESCAPED TO THE OTHER SIDE, RIGHT? THAT'S WHY *THIS* FELLOW IS HERE!

BUT WHY DID YOU COME *BACK* WITH HIM? THAT'S *NOT* PART OF THE PLAN!

UM...ER...

WELL...YA SEE, I'M *NOT* REALLY "YOUR" MICKEY! I'M JUST SOMEONE WHO - THANKS TO *MAGIC* - IS UNFORTUNATE ENOUGH TO *LOOK* LIKE HIM!

IF YER NOT *OUR* MICKEY, THEN THAT MEANS...

...YOU'RE *THEIR* MICKEY!

WE'RE *SAFE!* THEY CAN'T PASS THROUGH THE GLASS! BUT *WHY?*

AH! FIRST THEY MUST MAKE *EYE-CONTACT* WITH THEIR *REAL-WORLD COUNTERPARTS* - LIKE *WE* DID!

MARTY! WH-WHAT IS THIS ALL ABOUT?

CALL ME *MICKEY*, AND PERHAPS I'LL *TELL* YOU!

GRRR!

IT'S QUITE *AMAZING!* AFTER EYE-CONTACT IS MADE, THE MIRROR'S MAGIC GIVES BOTH A *PERSON* AND HIS *REFLECTION* THE POWER TO *TRAVEL* BETWEEN THEIR TWO WORLDS!

SO WHEN I TAKE *YOUR* FRIENDS HERE TOMORROW AND DUPE *THEM* INTO MAKING EYE-CONTACT, *MY* FRIENDS WILL BE FREE TO ENTER *YOUR* WORLD!

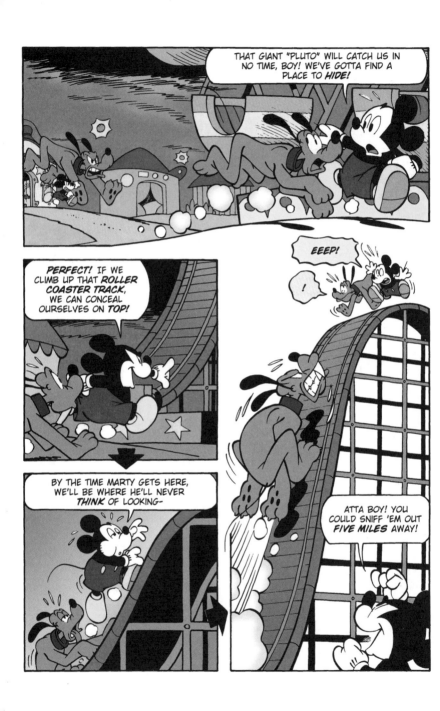

GET *OFF* OF US, YOU BIG MUTT! PUT US *DOWN!*

THAT'S IT! NOW TAKE THEM *BACK* TO THE MIRROR!

PHTTT!

I'LL TIE YOU UP HERE TILL TOMORROW! *THEN* - GAGGED TO ENSURE YOUR SILENCE - YOU'LL *SEE* WHAT HAPPENS TO YOUR *FRIENDS!* HA-HA!

BUT...*WHY?* WHY *WOULD* YOU WANT TO LEAVE YOUR *OWN* WORLD FOR OURS?

BECAUSE *OUR* WORLD IS ONLY A *REFLECTION*, AND WE *KNOW* IT! NONE OF US FEEL *REAL!* WE'RE ONLY *SHADOWS!*

NEED JELLY?

CLICK HERE

SCOOP

FOREVER'S A LONG TIME, MERLIN! I'LL *ESCAPE* FROM HERE SOMEDAY!

SHE *MIGHT!* I CAN'T DESTROY HER *MAGIC MIRROR!*

BUT MAYBE I CAN THINK OF *SOMETHING...*

HISSSS

...AND THIS IS THE *VERY MIRROR* FROM THE LEGEND!

ISN'T IT *THRILLING*, DONALD?

TINKLE

I *CHARMED* THE OWNER INTO DONATING IT TO MY CHARITY'S *AUCTION!*

THAT, AND THE *BELL OF MERLIN!*

SNORT!

SOME DONATION! A MIRROR *ENCRUSTED* WITH *CRUD...*

8

...AND A *BELL* WEDGED INTO A *STONE!*

WELL, IT'S ALL PART OF THE *LEGEND,* DONALD!

NOT *MORE* LEGEND? GROAN!

MERLIN DROVE THE BELL INTO THE STONE TO *PRESERVE* IT THROUGH TIME!

ONCE REMOVED, IT'S SUPPOSED TO LEAD ONE TO *MERLIN'S TOMB!*

YAWN!

NOTHING LIKE A *YARN* TO JACK UP THE PRICE OF THESE DUSTY DOODADS!

WELL, *I* HAPPEN TO BELIEVE THE LEGEND!

CHARITY AUCTION NEXT WEEK

BESIDES, IT'S FOR A *GOOD CAUSE* - AND *I* RAISED MORE ITEMS THAN *ANYONE!*

FOR CHARITY AUCTION

I'D THINK YOU MIGHT AT LEAST BE *PROUD* OF ME-

ZZZ

!?!

HUH? WHA'?

DON'T LET MY *WORK* KEEP YOU *AWAKE*, DONALD!

SORRY, DAISY - BUT THIS STUFF IS *BORING!*

BELLS YOU CAN'T RING AND MIRRORS YOU CAN'T USE...

...THEY'RE *WORTHLESS!*

EVEN IF ONE LED YOU TO *TREASURE?*

TREASURE?

IT'S A VALUABLE, FRAGILE *ANTIQUE!*

BUT...

...A *TREASURE!* YOUR *CHARITY* COULD SURE USE THE MONEY!

NO, DONALD!

NOW, *PLEASE* LET ME GET BACK TO WORK!

HM! THIS MIRROR *IS* FILTHY...

?

UNGH! URG! ARGH!

DONALD!

STOP IT!

OKAY, OKAY! IT WON'T *BUDGE* ANYWAY!

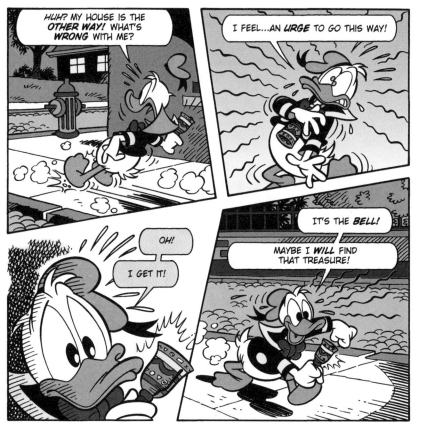

I'M SORRY, DAISY - BUT IT WAS JUST SO **TEMPTING!**

OF COURSE IT WAS!

I DON'T BLAME YOU FOR TAKING IT!

YOU **DON'T?** WHEW!

THEN, DAISY **FORGIVES** HER WIDDLE DONALD-POO?

!

THIS FOOL WANTS TO **KISS** ME! I'VE **NEVER** LET ANYONE DO THAT!

OH, WHAT THE HECK!

SMOOCH!!

SIGH!

WHAT TH-?!

CAD!

AT THE WATERFRONT...

I *MUST* BOARD THIS FREIGHTER!

BOUND FOR *ENGLAND!*

BUT WE HAVE NO MONEY!

THEN WE'LL *STOW AWAY!*

SOON...

WELL, THE CARGO HOLD ISN'T THE *RITZ*...

IT'LL DO, DONALD!

LET ME SEE THE BELL!

SURE...

YEOWCH!

WHAT'S WRONG?

I, EH... *CHANGED* MY MIND!

IT *BURNED* ME!

ZZT!

ONLY *HE* CAN BE GUIDED BY THE BELL! IT'S MERLIN'S *TRAP* TO LURE SOMEONE TO HIS TOMB!

ONCE THERE, MERLIN WILL BE *FREED* - IF THE BELL IS *RUNG THREE TIMES!*

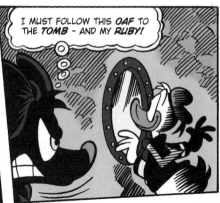

I MUST FOLLOW THIS *OAF* TO THE *TOMB* - AND MY *RUBY!*

AFTER *THAT* - HE'S EXPENDABLE!

ALL THIS EXERTION HAS *DEPLETED* ME! I MUST REST...

DAISY?! WHAT...

YOU *OKAY*, DAISY?

OH, DONALD! I MUST BE GOING *CRAZY!*

DUCKBURG...

CHARITY AUCTION NEXT WEEK

POOF!

HE'S RIGHT!

WHAT A GOOD IDEA!

MISS DAISY! IF WE *REINSTATE* YOU, WILL YOU BE OUR *"MISS BAD EXAMPLE"*?

GLADLY!

UH...NOW, DAISY...

PAY ATTENTION! HERE'S MY *FIRST DEMONSTRATION!*

TSK-TSK! SOME PEOPLE JUST HAVE NO *SELF-CONTROL!*

YOW!

MARVEL™ miniMates

They may be little, but they pack a full-sized punch!
Just when you thought your Mini Marvel Universe
couldn't expand any further, DST and Art Asylum
unleash two new series!

Series 10 will feature the following two-packs:
Sandman™ & Silver Sable™, Black Cat™ & Ben Reilly,
Spider-Carnage™ & Spider-Woman™,
and a Black Spider-Woman™ chase.

Series 11 features:
Bishop™ & Cable™, Rogue™ & Mystique™,
Firestar™ & Iceman™, and a clear Iceman™ chase.

SERIES 10 & 11

SILVER SABLE™

SANDMAN™

FIRESTAR™

ON SALE NOW!

www.marvel.com

www.diamondselecttoys.com

www.artasylum.com

cs.comic-book.com

MICKEY MOUSE IS A MEMBER OF THE EXPEDITION, TOO...

LET'S GO ON, THOR! I FEEL WE'RE CLOSE TO THE ANSWER!

MAYBE...BUT WE'LL SLEEP ON IT FOR NOW!

HOW CAN I SLEEP? THERE'S A MYSTERY TO SOLVE!

A WALK WILL RELAX ME!

THE STRANGE PHENOMENA HAVE BEEN DETECTED RIGHT IN THIS AREA...BUT WE HAVEN'T SEEN ANYTHING YET!

THEN...

HUH? THOSE SUDDEN FLASHES...MAYBE THAT'S IT!

AT THE FARMHOUSE, HE GETS A FRIENDLY WELCOME...

YOU DON'T KNOW HOW YOU GOT HERE? MAYBE A CHARIOT HIT YOU AND YOU LOST YOUR MEMORY...

UH...MAYBE! ALL I REMEMBER IS MY NAME... MICKEY!

SPEAKING OF...ER, CHARIOTS... ARE THEY SHOOTING A MOVIE AROUND HERE BY ANY CHANCE?

I DON'T THINK SO! WHY?

OH, NOTHING! SAY, WHO'S THAT?

ARE YOU SURE YOU FEEL ALL RIGHT?

THAT'S OUR EMPEROR... ROMULUS AUGUSTUS XXI!

OH, OF COURSE! HOW COULD I HAVE...ER, FORGOTTEN?

IT'S OBVIOUS YOU'VE SUFFERED A SHOCK!

GREAT CHIEF WISE EAGLE MAKES OFFICIAL VISIT TO MEET OUR EMPEROR

EDITORIAL

AVE!

PHOTO 6.8

MAYBE THERE WAS A HOLE BETWEEN DIMENSIONS...

...AND IT HURLED ME INTO A PARALLEL WORLD WHERE THE ROMAN EMPIRE NEVER FELL!

I'D BETTER PRETEND AMNESIA UNTIL I FIND OUT MORE!

MR. MICKEY!

THIS IS LUKE SCRIPTOR, A JOURNALIST FOR THE ROME TIMES! HE'LL TAKE YOU TO THE CITY!

UH... THANKS!

SOON...

EVERY SO OFTEN, I LIKE TO RELAX IN THE COUNTRY... SAY, WHO IS YOUR TAILOR?

I HOPE I CAN REMEMBER SOMEDAY!

HELP ME TO REMEMBER! WHAT'S THE CURRENT SITUATION WITH THE ROMAN EMPIRE?

EXCELLENT!

THE ECONOMY'S GOING GREAT... THE ROME STOCK MARKET IS SHOOTING UP!

AND THE EMPEROR? HE'S JUST A BOY...

HE ONLY HAS CEREMONIAL DUTIES! THE ACTUAL WORK IS DONE BY THE GOVERNMENT!

THAT ROMULUS IS A REAL PEST! AND NOW THAT HE HAS TO MEET WITH WISE EAGLE, EVERYONE IS CROSSING THEIR FINGERS!

WHY?

"AT THE LAST SUMMIT CONFERENCE, HE MADE EVERYONE WATCH ANIMATED CARTOONS FOR HOURS!"

THERE! THAT'S AMERICA!

NOT AT ALL! THAT'S CALLED BUFFALONIA...FROM THE ANIMALS IT'S MOST FAMOUS FOR! THERE ARE STILL HUGE HERDS OF THEM THERE!

AND NOBODY DISCOVERED IT! THEY CAME TO US ABOUT A THOUSAND YEARS AGO!

OH, YEAH?

SO IT WAS NEVER COLONIZED?

DO YOU THINK THEY WOULD HAVE LET US?

WE'VE HAD TRADE DISPUTES WITH THEM LATELY... BUT WISE EAGLE'S VISIT WILL RESOLVE THE PROBLEMS!

I'M CURIOUS ABOUT YOUR STRANGE MEMORIES... APPARENTLY THEY WERE SCRAMBLED BY THE SHOCK OF YOUR ACCIDENT!

BUT WHY DO THEY INTEREST YOU?

BECAUSE I'D LIKE TO BE A NOVELIST...IN THE FANTA-DEMENTIA GENRE!

FANTA...UH, DEMENTIA?

YES! IT'S A GENRE WITHOUT ANY LOGIC...IN WHICH ANYTHING IS POSSIBLE!

ALL RIGHT! THEN I'LL TELL YOU HOW AMERICA WAS DISCOVERED!

GREAT! LET'S GET STARTED! I'LL TAKE NOTES!

OKAY! CHRISTOPHER COLUMBUS WAS A NAVIGATOR WHO...

SOON...

IT'S COMPLETELY UNBELIEVABLE... BUT FASCINATING!

I'LL HAVE TO LEAVE OUT THE PART WHERE COLUMBUS THOUGHT HE WAS IN INDIA...IT'S TOO UNBELIEVABLE EVEN FOR FANTA-DEMENTIA!

YOUR CALL!

HOW WOULD YOU LIKE TO HELP ME WITH MY WORK UNTIL YOU GET YOUR MEMORY BACK?

GLADLY!

THOUSANDS OF YEARS OF CIVILIZATION...AND WE STILL HAVEN'T INVENTED CLOTHES MORE PRACTICAL THAN THESE TOGAS!

SAY! THAT'S SOMETHING NEW! WHO'S YOUR TAILOR?

UH...I DON'T KNOW!

AND WHO ARE YOU, BY THE WAY?

I DON'T KNOW THAT, EITHER!

ARE YOU PULLING MY LEG?

TAKE IT EASY, COMMISSIONER! WE'LL EXPLAIN EVERYTHING!

AFTER BEING BROUGHT UP TO DATE...

UHM...LET'S HOPE THAT YOU HAVEN'T RUN AFOUL OF THE LAW IN THE PAST!

I SEEM TO REMEMBER HAVING HELPED IT NOW AND THEN!

IT REALLY NEEDS SOME HELP NOW! I HAD TO PROVIDE SECURITY FOR THE SUMMIT CONFERENCE...

...AND I HAVE AN UNSOLVABLE CASE ON MY HANDS!

NO CASE IS UNSOLVABLE! IF YOU LIKE, WE COULD HELP YOU!

WE?

LET'S GO! THREE HEADS ARE BETTER THAN ONE!

THE CASE WOULDN'T BE IMPORTANT IF IT DIDN'T INVOLVE PUBLIUS COMICUS!

THE CREATOR OF SUPER-CAESAR? INCREDIBLE!

SUPER-CAESAR? WHO'S THAT?

THE HERO OF THE MOST POPULAR COMIC BOOK IN THE EMPIRE!

SUPER CAESAR

ON SALE TODAY - THE NEW ADVENTURE - SUPER-CAESAR VS. THE BARBARIANS FROM SPACE

EVERYBODY READS IT! EVEN COMMISSIONER OHARRICUS!

ONLY WITH MY NEPHEWS!

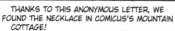

HAVE YOU ARRESTED HIM?

YES...THE EVIDENCE WAS AGAINST HIM, UNFORTUNATELY!

COME ON! THESE ARE HIS OFFICES...ALL THAT'S LEFT TO DO IS QUESTION MEA CULPA, HIS SECRETARY!

I DOUBT IF SHE CAN TELL US ANYTHING DECISIVE, BUT...

HOWEVER...

I HEARD PUBLIUS COMICUS ON THE TELEPHONE PROMISING SOMEBODY TO SELL HIM THE NECKLACE AS SOON AS HE HAD COLLECTED THE CLAIM MONEY FROM THE INSURANCE COMPANY!

AH HA! THAT'S THE PROOF WE NEEDED!

COMICUS SET THE WHOLE THING UP! ALONG WITH THE MONEY FROM THE INSURANCE COMPANY, HE ALSO WANTED THE MONEY FROM SELLING THE NECKLACE!

NOW THE CASE IS SOLVED!

YOU SAID IT! WE CAN GO!

LET'S NOT BE TOO HASTY!

?

IF SCRIPTOR COULD EXPLAIN TO ME HOW TO USE THIS...WE MIGHT BE ABLE TO FIND SOMETHING INTERESTING!

OF COURSE!

BUT THAT'S CRAZY! THE CASE IS CLOSED!

I JUST NEED HALF AN HOUR!

THERE'S A COLLECTION OF SUPER-CAESAR ADVENTURES! YOU CAN WHILE AWAY THE TIME WHILE WAITING!

I'VE READ THEM ALREADY!

THEN READ THEM AGAIN! COMICS ARE ENJOYABLE A SECOND TIME, TOO!

PHOOEY! I'VE ALREADY READ THEM THREE TIMES!

TIME PASSES AND...

WILL THIS TAKE MUCH LONGER?

NO...I'VE SEEN EVERYTHING I NEED TO!

WHAT'S MORE, YOU HAD ACCESS TO ALL OF YOUR EMPLOYER'S HOUSES...INCLUDING THE MOUNTAIN COTTAGE!

THE KEYS ARE IN THE OFFICE, OF COURSE!

AND YOU HAD AN AMBITION TO WRITE COMICS! YOU SUBMITTED YOUR STORIES TO COMICUS! THERE'S A FILE IN THE COMPUTER!

BUT HE REJECTED THEM...AND YOU WANTED TO GET REVENGE!

N-NO, I...

YOU STOLE THE NECKLACE, HIDING IT IN THE COTTAGE AND ALERTING THE POLICE WITH THE ANONYMOUS LETTER... WRITTEN HERE IN THE OFFICE!

SOB! IT'S TRUE! MY STORIES WERE BETTER THAN HIS BUT HE DIDN'T WANT TO ADMIT IT!

COME ALONG! I HAVE TO ARREST YOU!

I ALMOST PULLED IT OFF...SIGH!

LATER...

WHAT WOULD BE BETTER THAN A SUPER-CAESAR MOVIE TO CELEBRATE?

IT'S ALL VERY STRANGE..

WHAT'S THAT?

WHY DIDN'T COMICUS MENTION MEA CULPA'S BITTERNESS IN HIS TESTIMONY?

SO?

BECAUSE BEING ACCUSED OF THEFT WAS A BIG ENOUGH PROBLEM ALREADY AND HE DIDN'T WANT TO ATTRACT ATTENTION TO THE FILES ON HIS COMPUTER!

BESIDES, FOR BEING A PLOT OUTLINE... THOSE FILES CONTAINED TOO MUCH DETAIL ABOUT THE OPERATION!

LET'S GO ASK COMICUS A FEW QUESTIONS!

ALL RIGHT, BUT FIRST THERE'S SOMETHING WE CAN'T PUT OFF ANY LONGER!

SOON...

IT FITS YOU PERFECTLY... IT'S THE LATEST FASHION FROM BYZANTIUM!

AT LAST YOU'LL BE DRESSED LIKE YOU SHOULD BE!

THANKS!

AND SO...

I THANK YOU FOR YOUR HELP...YOU'VE CLEARED MY NAME!

GLAD TO! I'D JUST BE HAPPY TO SEE HOW SUPER-CAESAR STORIES ARE CREATED!

OF COURSE! COME INTO MY STUDIO!

THANKS!

DO YOU LIKE IT? THIS IS THE START OF A NEW STORY!

SUPERCAESAR and the ROBO-MINOTAUR

GREAT! BUT WHILE I WAS LOOKING FOR PROOF OF YOUR INNOCENCE, I SAW ANOTHER VERY INTERESTING STORY!

ANOTHER ONE? WHICH?

ABOUT SUPER-CAESAR AND WISE EAGLE!

OH, THAT! IT'S JUST AN OUTLINE...

A VERY DETAILED OUTLINE!

ALL RIGHT! YOU WIN! IT'S A SECRET BUT...COME WITH ME!

IT'S A SURPRISE STORY I'M PREPARING FOR THE SUMMIT CONFERENCE!

VERY INTERESTING!

I'M KEEPING THE FIRST PAGES IN MY SECRET STUDIO...

I'M EAGER TO SEE THEM!

LOOK! JUST GO BACK 902 YEARS! IT'S ALL DOCUMENTED!

SEE? THERE WAS AN ERROR HERE... MY ANCESTOR PUBLIUS OMITTERE SHOULD HAVE BEEN NAMED EMPEROR!

BUT THIS FAMILY TREE IS PHONY! IT WAS MADE BY "NOBILITY TO ORDER, INC.," A FRAUDULENT COMPANY!

FEH! DON'T SPLIT HAIRS!

WHAT ARE YOU GOING TO DO?

KIDNAP WISE EAGLE AND HOLD HIM PRISONER UNTIL ROMULUS ABDICATES!

YOU SHOULD GIVE YOUR-SELF UP INSTEAD! I HAVE A MICRO-TRANSMITTER LINKED STRAIGHT TO CHIEF OHARRICUS!

MICRO-WHAT?

A MICRO...UH...TRANS-MITTER! OHARRICUS HAS HEARD EVERYTHING AND WILL BE COMING HERE TO RESCUE US!

WHAT ARE YOU TALKING ABOUT?

JUST A PLAIN OLD MICRO-TRANSMITTER... A TINY GADGET THAT TRANSMITS SOUND!

HAH! PURE FANTA-DEMENTIA!

MICKEY, SUCH A DEVICE DOESN'T EXIST!

UH...I GUESS THINGS DIDN'T ALWAYS PROGRESS EXACTLY THE SAME WAY!

NEVER MIND THAT... IT LOOKS LIKE WE'RE IN SOME SERIOUS TROUBLE!

ANY IDEAS ON HOW TO ESCAPE?

YOU COULD PRETEND TO BE SICK, THE GUARDS WOULD COME RUNNING IN AND LIFT THE CAGE...

...OH, FORGET IT! IT'S SUCH AN OLD TRICK THAT...

ARE YOU KIDDING? IT'S A GREAT IDEA! AND THE FIRST I'VE HEARD OF IT!

WE CAN TRY! BUT IT SEEMS IMPOSSIBLE!

I'M JUST SORRY TO HAVE TO USE IT FOR REAL AND NOT SAVE IT FOR MY NOVEL!

THIS WORLD IS REALLY STRANGE! ALL RIGHT, LET'S DO IT!

AND SO...

OH! OW! IT HURTS! I CAN'T STAND IT! HELLPP!

WHAT'S GOING ON IN THERE? WE'D BETTER CHECK IT OUT!

QUICK! GET A DOCTOR! CAN'T YOU SEE HOW HE'S SUFFERING?

LIFT THE CAGE, SEMPRONIUS!

GET READY!

CLUUUNK CLANNG

WHAT'S WRONG WITH YOU?

STOMACHACHE, HE SAID...

...AND HERE'S ONE FOR YOU!

OOF!

THUMP

RUN FOR IT, SCRIPTOR!

THEY GOT ME! DON'T WORRY ABOUT ME – RUN!

THE FUTURE OF THE EMPIRE IS IN YOUR HANDS!

THIS ISN'T GOOD! WHAT CAN I DO ON MY OWN?

UH OH! THEY'VE ALREADY SOUNDED THE ALARM!

HE'S COMING FROM THERE! BLOCK THE EXITS!

SCREEEK

IF I CAN'T GO DOWN... I'LL GO UP!

GUARDS! GET HIM!

MAYBE THEY DIDN'T SEE ME RUN UP HERE...I COULD HAVE A LITTLE TIME!

HMM...IT'S SOME KIND OF STOREROOM! I WONDER IF I CAN FIND SOMETHING I CAN USE?

SOMEWHAT LATER...

DID YOU HAVE TO STUDY, CHIEF WISE EAGLE?

MUCH, MY BOY!

I'D RATHER WATCH ANIMATED CARTOONS!

AND IF MY TEACHER TELLS ME TO DO HOMEWORK... I FIRE HIM!

DON'T BELIEVE HIM! HE LOVES TO JOKE!

...AND BEFORE LONG, THINGS ARE BACK TO NORMAL...

THANKS AGAIN, MICKEY! YOU'VE SAVED THE EMPIRE!

AW, SHUCKS...IT WAS NOTHING! UH...COULD YOU HELP ME TAKE THESE WINGS OFF?

FLAP FLAP

AND SO, THE SUMMIT CONFERENCE IS SAVED... MORE OR LESS!

HA! HA! THAT JACOBUS BONDUS IS SO COOL!

JUST A FEW MORE MINUTES, YOUR EXCELLENCY...THEN WE'LL TALK ABOUT THE TREATY!

THE PLOTTER WINDS UP IN PRISON...

I'LL USE THE TIME TO INCREASE PRODUCTION OF SUPER-CAESAR!

GOOD IDEA! THAT'S YOUR TRUE CALLING!

...BUT FOR MICKEY, THINGS HAVEN'T CHANGED!

DON'T LOSE HEART! YOU'LL GET YOUR MEMORY BACK SOONER OR LATER!

SIGH! IF ONLY THAT WAS THE PROBLEM!

I NEVER LOST MY MEMORY, SCRIPTOR...AND NOW I WANT TO TELL YOU WHAT REALLY HAPPENED!

?

SOON...

WHAT A FASCINATING STORY...IT'S LIKE A WHOLE NOVEL! ALL THAT'S MISSING IS THE ENDING!

WHAT I'D LIKE IS TO WAKE UP AND REALIZE IT WAS ONLY A DREAM!

BUT NO ONE WOULD EVER END A STORY WITH SUCH A CLICHE!

CLICHE?

WHAT AN AMAZING SURPRISE ENDING! IT'LL REVOLUTIONIZE FICTION!

OH, REALLY?

IT HASN'T BEEN DONE ALREADY?

THIS'LL BE THE FIRST TIME, THANKS TO YOU! NOW TO PAY YOU BACK!

LET'S GO SEE MY FRIEND COSMO UNUSLAPIS! HE'S A GREAT PHYSICIST!

?

BEFORE LONG...

YOUR STORY CONFIRMS MY STUDIES...IT WAS A SPACE-TIME VORTEX THAT BROUGHT YOU HERE!

A VORTEX? DOES IT STILL EXIST?

I DON'T THINK SO! VORTICES USUALLY ONLY LAST A SHORT TIME BECAUSE THE ORDER OF THE UNIVERSE TENDS TO REESTABLISH ITSELF!

THEN...I'M DOOMED TO STAY HERE FOREVER?

NO! HERE YOU ARE A FOREIGN ELEMENT...

IT'S LIKELY THAT YOU'LL EVENTUALLY BE SENT HOME AUTOMATICALLY! IT COULD JUST TAKE A LITTLE WHILE!

HOW LONG?

A FEW CENTURIES, MORE OR LESS!

DON'T WORRY! WE HAVE LOTS OF WAYS TO PASS THE TIME AROUND HERE!

BUT THERE IS AN ALTERNATIVE! I HAVE INVENTED A DEVICE THAT SHOULD BE ABLE TO DETECT DIMENSIONAL VORTICES!

IT'S EXPERIMENTAL! I DON'T KNOW IF IT'LL WORK...

WHAT ARE YOU WAITING FOR? LET ME HAVE IT! I'LL EXPERIMENT WITH IT!

LATER...

COSMO SAID THAT VORTICES AREN'T RARE...BUT THEY DON'T LAST LONG!

SO WHEN YOU SEE ONE, YOU'LL HAVE TO JUMP IN IT RIGHT AWAY...

BEEP BEEP

...WITHOUT EVEN KNOWING WHERE YOU'LL END UP!

ACCORDING TO COSMO, I SHOULD GO BACK TO MY OWN SPACE AND TIME...ANYWAY, I'LL RISK IT!

I'M SORRY THAT YOU DON'T LIKE MY WORLD!

IT ISN'T THAT, YOU KNOW...

MEANWHILE, IN ANOTHER DIMENSION OF SPACE AND TIME...

MICKEY! WHERE HAVE YOU BEEN?

UH...I TOOK A WALK! DOES ANYBODY HAVE AN EXTRA PARKA? IT'S A LITTLE COLD OUT HERE!

SOON...

BUT WHY WERE YOU DRESSED LIKE AN ANCIENT ROMAN? WERE THE PENGUINS HAVING A COSTUME PARTY?

IT'S HARD TO EXPLAIN...

...SO I'LL JUST TELL YOU WE SHOULD GO BACK! THERE'S NOTHING MORE TO SEE NOW!

AT LEAST NOT UNTIL SOMETHING ACTIVATES THIS GADGET AGAIN...

LET'S BREAK CAMP! QUICK! WE HAVE TO TAKE MICKEY HOME...I DON'T THINK HE'S FEELING WELL!

END